Mary Ball Washington:

The Mother of George Washington

By

Michelle L. Hamilton

MLH Publications
12771 Camellia Drive
Ruther Glen VA 22546

Library of Congress Cataloging–in-Publication Data

Hamilton, Michelle L.
"*Mary Ball Washington: The Mother of George Washington*"

ISBN: 978-0-9995688-1-1

Copyright 2017

$\mathcal{M}$ary Ball Washington was born in Lancaster County, Virginia in 1708. Born into the Virginia gentry, Mary Ball's father Joseph Ball was a prominent landowner and respected member of the community. The Ball family had emigrated from England to the Virginia colony in 1650 settling in the Northern Neck.[1] Joseph Ball married Elizabeth Rogers (Romney) and had a son Joseph and several daughters. Following the death of Elizabeth Ball, Joseph Ball married Mary Johnson[2] Information about Mary Johnson is scarce. Mary Johnson was a widow and the mother of two children Elizabeth and John. Beyond that the records are silent.

The couple settled at Joseph Ball's plantation Epping Forest on the Rappahannock River. Joseph Ball died in 1711 when Mary was three years old.[3] In his will Joseph Ball left his daughter a legacy of 400 acres of land on the Rappahannock River at Little Falls Run, slaves, cattle, and enough feathers to make a feather bed. This inheritance would help the child establish herself within the Virginia gentry as she grew older. To provide for her children, Mary Johnson Ball married Richard Hughes.[4] Blended families in 18th-century Virginia was common, the average life expectancy for a woman was thirty-five years while the average life expectancy for a man was fifty years.

---

[1] Virginia Carmichael, *Mary Ball Washington* (Fredericksburg: Mary Washington Branch Association of the Preservation of Virginia Antiquities, 1987), 5.
[2] Paula S. Felder, *George Washington's Fredericksburg* (Virginia Beach: The Donning Company Publishers, 2011), 13.
[3] Ibid, 13.
[4] Ibid, 13.

Richard Hughes moved his wife and stepchildren to his plantation Cherry Point in Northumberland County. The marriage appeared to be happy and Richard Hughes was generous to his stepchildren. In the winter of 1713/1714, Richard Hughes died. In his will, Richard Hughes made his stepchildren the sole beneficiaries of his estate. Elizabeth Johnson received her stepfather's plantation Cherry Point and John Johnson received 600 acres in Stafford County. Mary's mother managed her late husband's estate and the family was able to stay together at Cherry Point.[5]

Mary Johnson Ball Hughes died in the winter of 1720. By the time Mary Ball was thirteen years old, her father, step-father, and mother had all passed away. Mary was well provided for by her mother. In her will, Mary Hughes appointed her son John Johnson and "my trusty and well-beloved friend, George Eskridge, executors of my last will and testament…And I do thereby appoint my daughter, Mary Ball, to be under tutelage and government of George Eskridge during her minority." To her youngest daughter, Mary Hughes bequeathed the following:

> "I give and bequeath to my daughter, Mary Ball, two gold rings, one being a large hoop, and the other a stoned ring…
>
> I give and devise to my daughter, Mary Ball, two diaper table cloths,[6] marked

---

[5] Ibid, 13.

[6] Diaper cloth was according to *Clothing and Fashion: American Fashion from Head to Toe,* "a twill weave fabric that is woven with lines crossing to form diamonds. The remaining spaces are lines, dots, or floral and

M.B. with ink, and two dozen of diaper napkins, two towels, six plates, and two pewter dishes…

I give unto my said daughter, Mary Ball, sufficient furniture for the bed her father, Joseph Ball, left her, namely; one set of good curtains and fallens, one rug, one quilt, and one pair of blankets.

I give and bequeath to my daughter, Mary Ball, one young likely negro woman to be purchased for her out of my estate and delivered unto her at the age of eighteen.

I give and devise to my daughter, Mary Ball, one mare and her increase which said mare I formerly gave her by word of mouth. I give and devise to my daughter, Mary

---

leaf patterns. The fabric was usually made of linen, but 18th-century linen cotton blends have surfaced. Diaper was used for summer waistcoats, bodices, and petticoats as well as table linens and household furnishings." José Blanco F. and Mary D. Doering, *Clothing and Fashion: American Fashion from Head to Toe: Volume One: Pre-Colonial Times through the American Revolution* (Santa Barbara: ABC-CLIO, 2016), 330.

Ball, one good young, pacing
horse, together with a good
silk plush saddle, to be
purchased by my executors
out of my estate."[7]

The winter of 1720 was tragic for Mary Ball. Shortly after the death of her mother, Mary's brother John Johnson died. Before his death, John Johnson left to his sister the 600 acres of land in Stafford County near the Accokeek mine that he had inherited from his stepfather Richard Hughes. Because of her late stepfather's generosity, Mary Ball remained at her childhood home Cherry Point where she lived with her sister Elizabeth and brother-in-law Samuel Bonum. George Eskridge served as Mary's legal guardian, by this time Mary had inherited about a thousand acres of land. The lawyer was also connected to Mary's family through marriage, as Samuel Bonum was the nephew of George Eskridge's first wife. The records suggest that Mary Ball was close with her sister and brother-in-law. Following Samuel Bonum's death in 1726 he left Mary "my young dapple gray rideing horse."[8]

George Eskridge helped Mary Ball manage her substantial land holdings and would introduce Mary to her husband. Augustine Washington was born in 1695 in Westmoreland County, Virginia. Orphaned at a young age, Augustine was a prominent land owner. In 1715, Augustine Washington married Jane Butler. The couple had four children. Along with managing his plantations, Augustine had become interested in iron ore mining and had begun buying land in Stafford County in partnership with the Principio Company in England. In the fall of 1729, Augustine

[7] Carmichael, *Mary Ball Washington,* 7-8.
[8] Felder, *George Washington's Fredericksburg,* 13.

traveled to England to negotiate a contract with the Principio Company located in Bristol, England. Augustine Washington took his surviving sons Lawrence and Augustine Jr. with him to enroll them at Appleby School in Whitehaven, Westmorland, England. Upon his return to Virginia in the spring of 1730, Augustine Washington received the devastating news that his wife had died during his absence. Occupied with the management of his plantations and his iron mine at Accokeek Creek in Stafford County, Augustine needed assistance to raise his daughter Jane.[9]

George Eskridge was a close friend of Augustine Washington and introduced him to Mary Ball. Augustine decided to remarry and courted Mary. On March 6, 1731 they were married at Yecomico Church in Westmoreland County. Mary was twenty-three years old; her husband was thirty-six years old. Augustine moved his wife to his plantation at Pope's Creek in Westmoreland County. Mary and Augustine Washington started their family quickly. On February 22, 1732, Mary gave birth to her first child George. Washington family legend claims that George was named for George Eskridge. In 1733, Mary gave birth to her second child, a daughter the family named Betty. The following year Mary gave birth to another son the family named Samuel. Life on Pope's Creek was difficult for the Washington family, in the winter of 1735, Jane Washington, Augustine's daughter, died at the age of twelve.

In 1735, Augustine Washington moved his growing family to his plantation at Little Hunting Creek (Mount Vernon). The family remained at Little Hunting Creek for three years. While living at Little Hunting Creek, Mary gave birth to two more sons, John Augustine in 1736 and Charles in 1738. During this period,

---

[9] Ibid, 11-13.

Augustine divided his time between managing his plantation and his iron mine. Management of the mine necessitated that Augustine had to frequently sail to England, leaving Mary in Virginia to raise the children and manage the plantations.[10]

Augustine Washington moved his family for a third time in the spring of 1738 to a plantation on the banks of the Rappahannock River in Stafford County across from Fredericksburg. The plantation was located near Augustine's mine and Mary's land holdings at Accokeek Creek. Augustine's sister Mildred Willis also lived nearby to the plantation that is known today as Ferry Farm.[11] In 1739, Mary gave birth to her last child, a daughter the family named Mildred. The Washington's time at Ferry Farm was difficult and was marred by misfortune. In October 1740, Mildred died from a childhood illness at the age of sixteen-months. This would not be the only misfortune that befell the family that year. On Christmas Eve a fire damaged part of the plantation house.[12]

In the spring of 1743, Augustine Washington became ill with a stomach disorder and wrote his will on April 11. The next day on April 12, 1743 Augustine Washington died after a short illness at the age of forty-nine.[13] Mary was thirty-five years-old, a widow with five children under the age of twelve to care for. With her husband's passing, Mary also lost sixty percent of her income on which to raise her children. Augustine's property was divided amongst his children. Lawrence and Augustine, Jr., Augustine Washington's oldest sons from his first marriage received their father's largest properties of Little Hunting Creek and Pope's

---

[10] Ibid, 16.
[11] Ibid, 18
[12] Ibid, 20
[13] Ibid, 20.

Creek respectively. George was his father's third son and he received the Ferry Farm property. Samuel, John Augustine, and Charles received 700 hundred acres of land to be divided between them. Betty received £400 on her eighteenth birthday and two female slaves.

Augustine Washington made provisions for his wife in his will leaving her the following items:

> "Item.—It is my will and desire that all the rest of my negroes not herein particularly devised may be equally divided between my wife and my three sons Samuel, John and Charles, and that Ned, Jack, Bob, Sue, and Lucy may be included in my wife's part, which part of my said wife's, after her decease I desire may be equally divided between my sons George, Samuel, John and Charles, and part of my said negroes so devised to my wife I mean and intend to be in full satisfaction and in lieu of her dower in my negroes. But if she should insist notwithstanding on her right of Dower in my negroes I will and desire that so many as may be wanting to make

up her share may be taken out of the negreos given hereby to my sons George, Samuel, John and Charles.

Item.—I give and bequeath unto my said wife and my four sons George, Samuel, John and Charles, all the rest of my Personal Estate to be equally divided between them which is not particularly bequeathed by this will to my wife and it is my will and desire that my said four sons Estates may be kept in my wife's hands until they respectively attain the age of twenty one years, in case my said wife continues so long unmarried but in case she Should happen to marry before that time I desire it may be in the power of my Executors to oblige her husband from time to time as they shall think proper to give security for the performance of this my last will in paying and delivering my said four sons their Estates respectively as they come of age, or on failure to give such security to take my said sons and their estates out of the custody and tuition of my said wife and her husband.

Item.—I give and bequeath unto my said wife the crops made at Bridge Creek, Chotank, and Rappahanock quarters at the time of my decease for the support of herself and her children and I desire my wife may have the liberty of working my land at Bridge Creek Quarters for the time of Five years next after my decease, during which time she may fix a quarters on Deeps Run."[14]

Mary Washington could have remarried as was common during the period. But in 18th-century Virginia, when a woman married, the property she brought into the marriage as her dowry would be controlled by her husband. Because Mary was serving in trust for her minor children, their property would be included with their mother's property under her dowry until they became of legal age. That meant that a new husband could make improvements to

---

[14] "The Will of Augustine Washington: Father to General George Washington," Mary Washington House archives.

the land, sell acreage, and have control of the revenue from the properties until the boys were legally adults. Augustine was so concerned about the welfare of his children after his death, that he included a clause in his will that his sons Lawrence and Augustine Jr., were to supervise the management of their half-brother's estates. If they were dissatisfied with the management of their brothers' properties they were to sue for custody and take the boys away from their mother. Mary decided to remain a widow and care for her children at Ferry Farm.

Mary Washington struggled financially to raise her children at Ferry Farm following the death of her husband. Due to the family's financial struggles, Mary was unable to send George and his younger brothers to England to receive their formal education, but he was educated in Fredericksburg by the Reverend James Marye. The Washingtons were members of the Church of England and attended St. George's Church in Fredericksburg. Mary also made sure that her children were schooled in social etiquette to insure that they could move amongst the gentry and make good marriages.[15]

George Washington was ambitious and was determined to make his mark on the world. Lawrence Washington urged Mary to allow George to join the British Navy. At first Mary Washington approved of the idea, but she decided to seek a second opinion and wrote to her older half-brother Joseph Ball who was a merchant in England. Joseph Ball wrote back to his sister advising her against the plan.

---

[15] For more information see Laura J. Galke, "The Mother of the Father of Our Country: Mary Ball Washington's Genteel Domestic Habits," *Northwest Historical Archaeology*, Vol. 38, 2009.

"I understand you are advis'd, and have Some Thoughts of putting your Son George to Sea. I think he had better be put aprentice to a Tinker; for a Common Sailor before the Mast, has by [n]o means the Common Liberty of the Subject; for they will press him from a Ship where he has 50. Shillings a month and make him take Three and twenty; and Cut & Slash him and use him like a Negro, or rather, like a Dog. And as for any Considerable Preferment in the Navy, it is not to be expected, there are So many always Gaping [grasping] for it here, who have Interest, and he has none. And if he Should get to be Master of a Virginia Ship (which will be very difficult to do) a Planter that has Three of four hundred Acres of Land, and Three or Four Slaves, if he be Industrious, may live more Comfortably, and Leave his Family in better Bread, than such a Master of a Ship can,"

Joseph Ball advised his sister
in 1746.[16]

Horrified by these reports of life in the British Navy, Mary retracted her consent and prevented George from joining the Navy. Mary was criticized by her associates for her decision. A family friend wrote to Lawrence and decried Mary's "trifling objections."[17] George Washington achieved his ambition for adventure at the age of sixteen when he became a surveyor mapping uncharted land in the Virginia colonies western territory.

Mary Washington's efforts to maintain the social position of the Washington family within the gentry were undermined by two social scandals that occurred at Ferry Farm. In the fall of 1750, one of the Washington's slaves Harry was placed on trial for the murder of a fellow Washington slave. The trial was recorded in the King George County court records on September 7, 1750,

"Harry a negro slave belonging to Mary Washington of this county— being brought ou[t] of goal and upon an Inditement arranged at the Bar for the murder of Negro Tame a man slave also belonging to the said Mary Washington Plead not guilty. The Court upon hearing the witnesses and duly considering the

---

[16] "Letter to Mary Washington from Joseph Ball (her half-brother), London, c. 1746," Mary Washington House archives.

[17] Felder, *George Washington's Fredericksburg*, 24.

case are of opinion that the sd [said] Negro Harry is guilty of the said murder said in the said inditment and thereuon do order that the said Harry do return to the Gaol from which he came, and the Sheriaf [Sheriff] on Wednesday the 10th day of October next, take him thence and carry him to the place of execution and then and there to hang him by the neck until he be dead."

The court valued Harry worth £35 and Mary Washington was reimbursed for the execution of her slave.[18]

Mary Washington had barely recovered from the social scandal of having a slave murder another slave on her plantation when the family was rocked by another embarrassing incident. In the summer of 1751, George Washington was bathing in the Rappahannock River when his clothes were stolen by two female indentured servants. The thieves were apprehended and one of the women received 15 lashes upon her bare back as punishment for her crime.[19] These events were embarrassing for Mary Washington who had sought to maintain a veneer of gentility at Ferry Farm.

[18] "King George County Records, Sept. 7, 1750," Mary Washington House archives.
[19] Galke, 35-36.

Fortunately for Mary the events did not have any lasting damage for her children's marital prospects.

When George Washington was twenty-one, his oldest half-brother Lawrence died leaving him the Mount Vernon plantation. George Washington also inherited his brother's position in the Virginia militia. In February 1753, George was appointed a major in the Virginia militia by Governor Robert Dinwiddie. Governor Dinwiddie sent George Washington to the Ohio Country to protect English interests from French and Native American incursion. During his time in the Ohio Country, Washington was ambushed by a French scouting party. During the ambush the French commander Joseph Coulon de Jumonville was killed. Jumonville's death sparked the French and Indian War. Young Major Washington would play a leading role in the French and Indian War.

In the summer of 1755, George Washington was stationed in the Pennsylvania frontier under General Edward Braddock. George Washington kept his mother apprised of his location.

> "I was favoured with your Letter by Mr Dick, and am sorry it is not in my power to provide you with a Dutch Servant, or the Butter agreeably to you[r] desire, We are quite out of that part of the Country where either are to be had, there being few or no Inhabitants where we now lie Encamped, & butter cannot be had here to supply

the wants of the army," George wrote to his mother on June 7, 1755.[20]

The next month on July 9, 1755, General Edward Braddock's forces were ambushed by French and Native American forces at the Battle of Monongahela. The battle was a disaster for the British and Colonial forces, but George Washington was signaled out for his bravery under fire. Writing to his mother on July 18, 1755, George wrote,

> "I luckily escaped witht [without] a wound, tho' I had four Bullets through my Coat, and two Horses shot under me; Captns Orme & Morris two Aids de Camps, were wounded early in the Engagemt which renderd the duty harder upon me, as I was the only person then left to distribute the Genls Orders, which I was scarcely able to do, as I was not half recovered from a violent illness that had condfin'd me to my Bed, and a Waggon,

---

[20] "From George Washington to Mary Ball Washington, 7 June 1755," Founders Online, https://founders.archives.gov/?q=%20Author%3A%22Washington%2C%20Ge orge%22%20mary%20ball%20washington%20Recipient%3A%22Washington %2C%20Mary%20Ball%22&s=1111311111&r=2 (accessed October 26, 2017).

for above 10 Days; I am still
in a weak and Feeble condn
[condition] which induces
me to halt here 2 or 3 Days in
hopes of recovg a little
Strength, to enable me to
proceed homewards; from
whence, I fear I shall not be
able to stir towards Sepr
[September], so that I shall
not have the pleasure of
seeing you till then…"[21]

In January 1759, George Washington married Martha Dandridge Custis, the wealthiest widow in Virginia. Also in 1759, George Washington resigned from the Virginia militia, to the relief of his mother. "There was no end to my troble [trouble] while George was in the army butt he has now given it up," Mary Washington wrote to her brother in England on July 26, 1759.[22] In 1761 George Washington wanted his mother to move to Fredericksburg to be nearer her daughter Betty Lewis who had married her distant cousin, Fielding Lewis, in 1750. Mary Washington had dower rights to Ferry Farm, which meant that she could live there for the rest of her life if she never remarried. Mary

[21] "From George Washington to Mary Ball Washington, 18 July 1755," Founders Online, https://founders.archives.gov/?q=%20Author%3A%22Washington%2C%20Ge orge%22%20mary%20ball%20washington%20Recipient%3A%22Washington %2C%20Mary%20Ball%22&s=1111311111&r=3 (accessed October 26, 2017).
[22] "Transcript Mary Washington to Joseph Ball July 26, 1759," Mary Washington House archives.

was content and did not wish to move, and her son had to abandon his plan.[23]

Mary Washington continued to live at Ferry Farm until the early 1770s. Mary Washington was in her early sixties and had lived twice the average life expectancy. Her five children had all married and had moved away from home. Two of her children lived in Fredericksburg. Her youngest son, Charles lived on Caroline Street at the property now known as the Rising Sun Tavern. Fielding Lewis was overseeing the construction of his planation that is now known as Kenmore. Mary still lived at Ferry Farm. Traveling to Fredericksburg was difficult, as a bridge across the Rappahannock River had not been constructed yet. Her physicians, including Dr. Hugh Mercer were also located in Fredericksburg. Her children were concerned about her welfare.

In the winter of 1771, Mary fell ill with the influenza.[24] Betty could not come to nurse her mother as she was recovering from childbirth.[25] After Mary recovered, she saw the advantage of living in town near her adult children. But she was a strong, independent woman and did not want to live with her adult children—she wanted her own establishment. George Washington placed Ferry Farm up for sale and purchased his mother a property in town. The cottage was one and a half stories. It was situated on two half acre lots that was owned by Michael Robinson, who had made his living as a tobacco inspector. George Washington paid

---

[23] Galke, 32.

[24] Doctor Hugh Mercer Ledger, Hugh Mercer Apothecary Shop archives.

[25] Paula S. Felder, *Fielding Lewis and the Washington Family: A Chronicle of 18th Century Fredericksburg* (American History Company, 1998), 73.

£275 for the property.[26]   The house and lots was next to the Lewis plantation.   Michael Robinson deeded the property to George Washington on September 18, 1772.[27]   Mary Washington had already moved into the property in April 1772 before it was officially transferred to George Washington.

Shortly after she moved in, George Washington visited her in her new home. On April 11, 1772, George Washington recorded in his journal, "Breakfasted at Hubbard's and dined at Colo. Lewis's in Fredericksburg…I lodged at my Mothers."[28] Before the Revolutionary War, George Washington visited his mother and his family in Fredericksburg several times a year. In the pages of his journal, George Washington recorded visiting and dining with his mother frequently between 1772 through 1775. During this period, George Washington helped his mother financially and purchased her gifts. On October 24, 1774, George Washington recorded in his ledger a payment to "Phil Marchinton of Phila. For £10.2.1 a Cloak lind [lined] with silk Shag," for his mother.[29]

By 1774, the threat of war with Great Britain had become apparent in Fredericksburg. Following the Tea Act of 1773 many residents of Fredericksburg stopped drinking tea and buying products from the East India Company. Fredericksburg resident John Harrower wrote to his wife in Scotland on June 14, 1774,

---

[26] Ibid, 166.
[27] Note on George Washington journal entry for November 8, 1771 journal, Founders Online https://founders.archives.gov/?q=%20Author%3A%22Washington%2C%20George%22%20November%201771&s=1111311111&r=20 (accessed October 26, 2017).
[28] Felder, *George Washington's Fredericksburg*, 65.
[29] The Financial Papers of George Washington, Ledger B, 1772-1793, pg. 45, http://financial.gwpapers.org/?q=content/ledger-b-1772-1793-pg45 (accessed October 26, 2017).

"As for Tea there is none drunk by any in this Government since 1st. June last, nor will they buy a 2d. worth of any kind of east India goods, which is owning to the difference at present betwixt the Parliament of great Brittan [Britain] and the North Americans about laying a tax on the tea; and I'm afraid if the Parliament do not give it over it will cause a total revolt as all the North Americans are determined to stand by one another, and resolute on it that they will not submit."[30]

Despite the boycott on tea, Mary Washington continued to drink her favorite brew. On May 18, 1774 Mary Washington paid Robert Broom 18 shillings for Hyson tea.[31]

In April 1775 the Revolutionary War began at the Battles of Lexington and Concord. George Washington was elected Commander in Chief of the rag tag Continental Army. Communication between George Washington and his family

[30] "The Diary of John Harrower," The Colonial Williamsburg Foundation, http://www.history.org/history/teaching/enewsletter/volume3/may05/primsource.cfm (accessed October 26, 2017).
[31] "Receipt—Robert Broom to Mrs. Mart Washington, May 18, 1774," Mary Washington House archives.

during the Revolutionary War was difficult. The challenges of mailing letters to camp and the risk of personal correspondence falling into British hands limited George Washington's contact with his family in Fredericksburg. On March 30, 1778, Brigadier General George Weedon updated his commander on the state of his family in Fredericksburg:

> "Colo. Lewis is just returned from the Country where he has been under Innoculation, has had a very favourable time during the Disorder and is perfectly recovered. Mrs Lewis was unfortunate enough to take it in the natural way during his absence, She however has it but slightly and will soon be about again, Mrs Washington underg[oes] great uneasiness for fear she should take it, She cannot be persuaded to Innoculate, tho' it has been, and is now in almost every House in Town & Country."[32]

---

[32] "To George Washington from Brigadier General George Weedon, 30 March 1778," Founders Online, https://founders.archives.gov/?q=george%20weedon%2030%20march%201778%20Recipient%3A%22Washington%2C%20George%22%20Author%3A%2Weedon%2C%20George%22&s=1111311111&sa=&r=1&sr= (accessed October 26, 2017).

Mary Washington's fears of smallpox inoculation were well founded, as many patients died during the inoculation process.

The Revolutionary War presented a series of economic and personal hardships for Mary Washington. After the smallpox epidemic, the region experienced a poor harvest, which resulted in food and cash being in short supply for Mary. On December 9, 1778, Mary Washington was forced to write to Lund Washington at Mount Vernon for relief. During her sons absence from Mount Vernon, Lund Washington, a cousin, had been overseeing the management of the plantation.

> "I should much obliged to you to send me forty pound cash to by corn for tho have not maid [made] more at the Little falls quarter then will sarve [serve] the plantation thear is terruable doings thiur Charls never goes over I shall be ruined corn at five pound a barel as for flower [flour] I dont know the tast[e] of it i never lived soe pore in my life butt if I can qitt [get] corn I am Contented pray send the cash by some safe hand for I have no one to send butt a Negro [unclear] doe these sharp times I hear pore Mrs Washington is [unclear] of God bles you and spar your

health as pore George will be ruined I am Dear Lund your fond kinswoman," Mary begged in her letter.[33]

Within weeks, Mary Washington received the financial assistance from Mount Vernon. "Jest as I had wrote to you not [t]o send Cash by overseer Con'l Bassett came in and delivered the forty pound Cash to me from you and am Dear Sir you[r] most affectinat humble servant," Mary Washington wrote to Lund Washington on December 23, 1778.[34]

The personal and financial hardships would be present in Mary Washington's life throughout the entirety of the Revolutionary War. In 1780, twenty-five pounds of bacon was impressed by the government to feed the Continental soldiers in the field.[35] During this period, Mary Washington wrote to her son John Augustine Washington in an undated letter:

"My dear Johnne,

I am very glad to hear you and all the family is well and should be glad if I could writ you the same.

I am a going fast and it be time as hear I am borring a Little Corn no Corn

---

[33] "Transcript Mary Washington to Lund Washington, December 9, 1778," Mary Washington House archives.

[34] "Transcript Mary Washington to Lund Washington, December 23, 1778," Mary Washington House archives.

[35] Felder, *Fielding Lewis and the Washington Family*, 276.

in the Cornhous I Never Lived soe por [poor] in my Life was i[t] not for Mrs. French and your Sister Lewis I should be almost starved butt I am like an old almanac quit [quite] out of date give my Love [to] Mrs. Washington and all the family and am Dear Johnne

your Loving and affect. Mother

Mary Washington

P.S. I should be glad to see you as I Dont expect to hold it long[.]"[36]

Mary Washington has been accused by modern historians of having Loyalist sympathies during the Revolutionary War based on the account of the Comte de Clermont-Crèvecoeur who passed through Fredericksburg in 1782. The Comte recorded in his diary on July 14, 1782, "Fredericksburg is where General Washington's mother lives. We went to call on her but were amazed to be told that this lady, who must be over seventy, is one of the most rabid Tories. Relations must be very strained between her and her son, who will always be the right arm of American freedom."[37]

---

[36] "Transcript Mary Washington to John Augustine Washington, undated," Mary Washington House archives.
[37] Howard C. Rice, Jr. and Anne S. K. Brown, *The American Campaigns of Rochambeau's Army 1780, 1781, 1782, 1783: Volume I: The*

Shocked by this account the soldiers decided to not pay a visit to Mary Washington. Comte de Clermont-Crèvecoeur failed to provide any evidence for this allegation.

Mary Washington received her most distinguished guest in April 1781. Marie-Joseph Paul Yves Roch Gilbert du Motier, Marquis de Lafayette was sent by General Washington to Maryland on military business. On his route, the Marquis de Lafayette passed through Fredericksburg and could not resist the opportunity to meet General Washington's family. "I Myself Hastened Back to Maryland, But I Confess Could Not Resist the Ardent desire I Had long Ago of Seeing Your Relations And Above All your Mother at Frederisk Burg—For that purpose I Went Some Miles out of the Way, and in order to Conciliate My Private Happiness to duties of a Public Nature, I Recovered By Riding in the Night those few Hours Which I Had Consecrated to My Satisfaction," the Marquis de Lafayette wrote to his commander on April 8, 1781.[38] The Marquis de Lafayette remained fond of Mary Washington for the remainder of her life. On February 5, 1783 the Marquis wrote to George Washington, "Be so kind My dear General, to Remember me to Your Much Respected Mother—Her Happiness I Heartly Partake."[39] Even Adrienne, Marquise de Lafayette expressed her fond regard for Mary Washington in her letters to George Washington. "My Mother will receive the

Journals of Clermont-Crèvecoeur, Verger, and Berthier (Princeton: Princeton University Press, 1972), 73.

[38] "To George Washington from Marie-Joseph-Paul-Yves-Roch-Gilbert du Motier, marquis de Lafayette, 8 April 1781," Founders Early Access, http://rotunda.upress.virginia.edu/founders/default.xqy?keys=FOEA-print-01-01-02-5335 (accessed October 26, 2017).

[39] "To George Washington from Marie-Joseph-Paul-Yves-Roch-Gilbert du Motier, marquis de Lafayette, 5 February 1783," Founders Early Access, http://rotunda.upress.virginia.edu/founders/default.xqy?keys=FOEA-print-01-02-02-4575 (accessed October 26, 2017).

Compliments you honor her with, as a flattering mark of your attention; & I shall have great pleasure in delivering them myself," George Washington wrote to the Marquise on May 10, 1786.[40]

In the spring of 1781 during the British invasion of Virginia, Fredericksburg was placed under alert. Concerned that the British would capture Mary Washington and her family, General George Weedon ordered the Washington and Lewis family to move to a place of safety until the crisis had passed.[41] Mary Washington went with Betty and Fielding Lewis to their land holdings in Frederick County. The family's residence in Frederick County, Virginia was difficult, Fielding Lewis was dying from a lung complaint and the housing for the family was cramped.

During this difficult time, Mary Washington attempted to improve her financial stability by applying for a pension from the Virginia legislature based on services her late husband Augustine Washington had provided to the colony. The news that his mother had applied for a pension did not sit well with her son. George Washington viewed this as a public declaration that he was finically neglecting her. George Washington sent a blistering letter to legislator Benjamin Harrison on March 21, 1781:

> "I do not delay a
> moment to thank you for the
> interesting matter contained
> in it, and to express my
> surprize at that part which

[40] "From George Washington to Adrienne, Marquise de Lafayette, 10 May 1786," Founders Online, https://founders.archives.gov/?q=Adrienne%2C%20Marquise%20de%20Lafay ette%2C%2010%20may%201786&s=1111311111&sa=&r=3&sr= (accessed October 26, 2017).

[41] Felder, *Fielding Lewis and the Washington Family*, 298-299.

respects a pension for my Mother.

True it is, I am but little acquainted with her present situation, or distresses, if she is under any. As true it is, a year or two before I left Virginia (to make her latter days comfortable, & free from care) I did, at her request but at my own expense purchase a commodious house, Garden & Lotts (of her own choosing) in Fredericksburg, that she might be near my Sister Lewis, her only daughter—and did moreover agree to take her Land & Negroes at a certain yearly rent, to be fixed by Colo. Lewis & others (of her own nomination,) which has been an annual expense to me ever since, as the Estate never raised one half the rent I was to pay—Before I left Virginia, I answered all her calls for money; and since that period, have directed my Steward to do the same.

Whence her distresses can arise therefore, I know not, never having received any complaint of his inattention or neglect on that head; tho 'his inability to pay my own taxes being the most unequal (I am told) in the world— some persons paying for things of equal value, four times, nay ten times, the rate that others do. But putting these things aside, which I could not avoid mentioning, in exculpation of a presumptive want on my part; confident I am that she has not a child that would not divide the last sixpence to relieve her from real distress. This she has been repeatedly assured of by me: and all of us, I am certain, would feel much hurt, at having our mother a pensioner, while we had the means of supporting her; but in fact she has an ample income of her own.

I lament exceedingly that your letter, which conveyed the first

hint of this matter, did not
come to my hands sooner;
but I request, in pointed
terms if the matter is now in
agitation in your assembly,
that all proceedings on it
may be stopped—or in case
of a decision in her favor,
that it may be done away, &
repealed at my request…"[42]

While in Frederick County, Mary Washington missed seeing her son George Washington for the first time since 1775 when he passed through town on September 13, 1781 en route to Yorktown. Fielding Lewis succumbed to his illness on December 7, 1781. Mary Washington finally returned to her home early in 1782. Mary Washington expressed her distress on not being able to see George Washington in a letter to him on March 17, 1782:

"My Dear Georg

I was truly unsy
[uneasy] My Not being at
ho[me] when you went throu
fredericksburg it was an un
[unclear] pleasure for me
now I am afraid I never shall
have that [unclear] pleasure
agin I am soe very unwell &
this trip over the Mountains

---

[42] Edward G. Lengel, *This Glorious Struggle: George Washington's Revolutionary War Letters* (Washington, D.C.: Smithsonian Books, 2007), 226-227.

has almost killed me I gott
the 20 five ginnes [guineas]
you was soe kind to send me
& am greatly obliged to you
for it I was greatly shockt
[shocked] [unclear]…

…ever be driven up
this way by me [unclear] will
goe in some little hous
[house] of my one [own] if it
is [unclear] twelve fott [foot]
squar…you pray give my
kind Love to Mrs.
Washington & am My Dear
George your

Loveing & affectinat
[affectionate] Mother[.]"[43]

Mary Washington was an active presence in her community. Neighbor William Simmes wrote about Mary Washington in a June 23, 1783 letter to his family:

"I have the honour to
live within some yards of
Gen. Washington's sister,
the widow Lewis—a fine
figure of an old lady as ever
I have seen. But what is
more, I have his mother on

---

[43] "Transcript, Mary Washington to George Washington, March 13, 1782," Mary Washington House archives.

the other side about the same distance—and older lady no doubt, but equally active & sprightly notwithstanding. She goes about the neighborhood to visit our quality on foot, with a cane in her hand & sometimes a Negro girl walking behind her to assist her in case of necessity.

She must be near eighty years old—& talks of George without the least pride or vanity. She will not keep any carriage, but a chair and two old family horses…She lives in a little house of one story without the least affectation of magnificence. The front windows are always shut & barred—for she delights to live in a little back room or two where I have seen her sitting at work with a slave to attend her—such is her taste."[44]

---

[44] "Transcript of William Simmes letter, June 23, 1783," Mary Washington House archives

When the distance was too great to walk, Mary Washington would travel in her riding chair a sight that would be remembered by those who knew her. "There are some of the aged inhabitants of Fredericksburg who well remember the matron as, seated in an old-fashioned open chaise, she was in the habit of almost daily visiting her little farm in the vicinity of the town...," George Washington Parke Custis recalled in his memoir.[45]

In 1859, a correspondent from the *Lowell* [Massachusetts] *Daily Citizen* recorded his interview with a neighbor of Mary Washington. "There are those still living here who are able to speak from their personal recollections of 'Mary, the mother of Washington.' A venerable lady with whom I have been talking tells me that she can distinctly recall her short, rather thick-set figure, and her peculiar round straw hat and red cloak, as in her childhood she was accustomed to see the old lady stirring around the neighborhood. The traditions are that she was not remarkable for amenities of character, but rather for method and order, strict house hold government, and decision of purpose."[46]

With the conclusion of the Revolutionary War, George Washington returned to Fredericksburg to visit his mother in February 1784. George Washington had planned on visiting his mother earlier in the year, but had been hampered by bad weather. "We have been so fast locked in Snow and Ice since Christmas, that all kinds of intercourse have been suspended; and a duty which I owed my Mother, and intended 'ere this to have performed, has been forced to yield to the intemperance of the Weather: but, as this again must submit to the approaching Sun, I shall soon be enabled,

[45] George Washington Parke Custis, *Recollections and Private Memoirs of Washington* (New York: Derby & Jackson, 1860), 139-140.
[46] "Washington's Mother," *Lowell Daily Citizen and News*, December 2, 1859, Fredericksburg and Spotsylvania National Military Park archives.

I expect, to discharge that duty on which Nature and inclination have a call," George Washington wrote to his friend Charles Thomson on January 22, 1784.[47]

Mary Washington had not seen her son since the start of the war in 1775. During the visit, George Washington was lauded by Mayor William McWilliams and the city council who publically praised Washington for his, "long and meritorious services in the cause of liberty, [whereby] the virtuous citizens of the western world are secured in freedom and independence."

The February 21, 1784 edition of the *Virginia Gazette* reprinted George Washington's official response to Mayor McWilliams and the city council's welcoming remarks:

"To the Worshipful Mayor, and the Commonalty of the Corporation of Fredericksburg,

"Gentlemen,

With the greatest of pleasure I receive, in the character of a private citizen, the honor of your address. To a benevolent Providence, and the fortitude of a brave and virtuous army, supported by the general exertion of our

---

[47] Thomas J. Fleming, *Affectionately Yours, George Washington: A Self-Portrait in Letters of Friendship* (New York: W.W. Norton & Company, 187.

common country, I stand indebted for plaudits you now bestow.

The reflection, however, of having me the congratulating smiles and approbation of my fellow citizens...cannot fail of adding pleasures to the other sweets of domestic life; and my sensibility of them is heightened by their coming from the respectable inhabitants of the place of my growing infancy, and the honourable mention which is made of my revered mother, by whose maternal hand, early deprived of a father I was led to manhood..."[48]

In the years following the Revolutionary War, George Washington was able to visit his mother frequently as he had been able to do before the war. On April 29, 1785, George Washington recorded in his diary, "Dined at Dumfries, and lodged at my Sister Lewis's (after visiting my Mother) in Fredericksburg." Before returning to Mount Vernon, Washington visited his mother a few days later on May 5, 1785. "Dined with my Sister Lewis in

---

[48] Felder, *George Washington's Fredericksburg*, 68.

Fredericksburg, spent half an hour with my Mother...," George Washington recorded in his journal.[49]

In the winter of 1787, John Augustine Washington died at his home in Mount Holly, Virginia. This was the second son Mary Washington lost in the 1780s, in 1781 Samuel Washington died at his plantation in Berkeley County, Virginia [West Virginia]. The death of John Augustine shocked his family. "John...whoes death I sincerely lament on many Accounts and on this painful event condole with you most sincerely," George Washington wrote to his mother on February 15, 1787.[50]

By 1787, George Washington was financially strapped and was finding it difficult to support his mother. Reports had reached George Washington that he had been accused of being a bad son for not providing for his mother. This accusation was deeply offensive to George Washington who valued his reputation as an honorable member of the gentry. George had also become frustrated with reports that the planation at Little Falls was being mishandled. On February 15, 1787, George Washington vented his frustration to Mary Washington:

> "Further, my sincere,
> and pressing advice to you is,
> to break up housekeeping,
> hire out all the rest of the
> servants except a man and a
> maid and live with one of

---

[49] Ibid, 69.

[50] "From George Washington to Mary Ball Washington, 15 February 1787," Founders Online, https://founders.archives.gov/?q=Mary%20Washington%20%20Author%3A%22Washington%2C%20George%22%201787&s=1111311111&sa=&r=47&sr=%20 (accessed October 26, 2017).

your Children. This would relieve you entirely from the cares of the world, and leave your mind at ease to reflect, undisturbedly on that which aught to come. On this subject I have been full with my Brother John and it was determined he should endeavor to get you to live with him—He alas is no more & three only of us remain—My House is at your service, & would press you most sincerely & most devoutly to accept it, but I am sure and candour requires me to say it will never answer your purposes, in any shape whatsoever—for in truth it may be compared to a well restorted tavern, as scarcely any strangers who are going from north to south, or from south to north do not spend a day or two at it—This would, were you to be an inhabitant of it, oblige you to do one of 3 things, 1st to be always dressing to appear in company, 2d to come into in a dishabille or

3d to be as it were a prisoner in your own chamber The first yould not like, indeed for a person at your time of life it would be too fateiguing. The 2d I should not like because those who resort here are as I observed before strangers and people of the first distinction. and the 3d, more than probably, would not be pleasing to either of us—nor indeed could you be retired in any room in my house; for what with the sitting up of Company; the noise and bustle of servants—and many other things you would not be able to enjoy that calmness and serenity of mind, which in my opinion you ought now to prefer to every consideration in life. If you incline to follow this advice the House and lotts on which you now live you may rent, and enjoy the benefit of the money arising there from as long as you live—this with the rent of the land at the little falls & the hire of your negroes would bring you in an income which would be much more than sufficient to answer all your wants and make ample amends to the child you live with; for myself I should desire nothing, if it did not, I would, most cheafully contribute more. a man, a maid, The Phaeten [phaeton carriage] and two horses, are all you would want—to lay in a sufficiency for the support of these would not require ¼ of your income, the rest would purchase every necessary you could possibly want, and place it in your power to be serviceable to those with whom you may live, which no doubt, would be agreeable to all parties.

There are such powerful reasons in my mind for giving this advice, that I cannot help urging it with a degree of earnestness which is uncommon for me to do. It is I am convinced, the only means by which you can be happy. the cares of a family without any body to assist you—The charge of an estate the proft of which depend upon wind weather—a good Overseer—an honest man—and a thousand other circumstance, cannot be right, or proper at your advanced age & for me, who am absolutely prevented from attending to my own plantations which are almost within call of me to attempt the care of yours would be folly in the extreme; but the mode I have pointed out, you may reduce your income to a certainty, be eased of all trouble—and, if you are so disposed, may be perfectly happy—for happiness depends more upon the internal frame of a persons own mind—than on the externals in the world. of the last if you will pursue the plan here recommended I am sure you can want nothing that is essential—the other depends wholy upon your

self, for the riches of the
Indies cannot purchase it."[51]

By the late 1780s, Mary Washington's health had begun to deteriorate. In the final years of her life, Mary was diagnosed with breast cancer. In April 1787, Mary Washington became dangerously ill. Concerned that she was dying, George Washington was summoned to her bedside. "Thursday, 26th. Receiving an Express between 4 and 5 Oclock this afternoon informing me of the extreme illness of my Mother and Sister Lewis, I resolved to set out for Fredericksburg by daylight in the morning," George Washington recorded in his journal.[52] Before departing Mount Vernon, George Washington penned a letter to Henry Knox regarding a planned trip to Philadelphia to attend a convention.

"And tho' so much afflicted
with a rheumatic complaint
(of which I have not been
entirely free for Six months)
as to be under the necessity
of carrying my arm in a sling
for the last ten days, I had
fixed on Monday next for my
departure, and had made
every necessary arrangement
for the purpose when (within
this hour) I am summoned by
an express who assures me
not a moment is to be lost, to

[51] Ibid.
[52] Felder, *George Washington's Fredericksburg*, 70.

see a mother, and *only* Sister (who are supposed to be in the agonies of death) expire; and I am hastening to obey this melancholy call, after having just bid an eternal farewell to a much loved Brother who was the intimate companion of my youth and the most affectionate friend of my ripened age," Washington wrote on April 27, 1787.[53]

Rushing to Fredericksburg, George Washington was relieved to find that the dire pronouncement delivered the day before had been exaggerated. "Friday, 27th. About sun rise I commenced my journey as intended. Bated at Dumfries, and reached Fredericksburg before two Oclock and found both my Mother and Sister better than I expected. The latter out of danger as is supposed, but the extreme low State in wch. [which] the former was left little hope of her recovery as she was exceedingly reduced and much debilitated by age and the disorder," George Washington recorded in his journal.[54]

In May of 1788, Mary Washington wrote her will. A month later in June 1788, George and Martha Washington paid Mary a

---

[53] "From George Washington to Henry Knox, 27 April 1787," Founders Online, https://founders.archives.gov/?q=Mary%20Washington%20%20Author%3A%22Washington%2C%20George%22%201787&s=1111311111&sa=&r=50&sr=%20 (accessed October 26, 1789).

[54] Felder, *George Washington's Fredericksburg*, 70.

visit. "Tuesday, 10th. Between 9 and 10 Oclock set out for Fredericksburg accompanied by Mrs. Washington, on a visit to my Mother," George Washington wrote in his journal. The next day, June 11, 1788, the Washingtons arrived in Fredericksburg, "alighted at my Mother's and sent the Carriage and horses to my Sister Lewis's, where we dined and lodged."[55]

By 1789, Mary's health was rapidly deteriorating. On the eve of being elected President of the United States, George Washington was preparing for the summons to New York City to be sworn in. In the midst of settling his affairs, George Washington prepared to visit Fredericksburg to say farewell to his mother. Writing to Richard Conway about a business arrangement, Washington wrote on March 6, 1789, "...I would have done it this day but being to set of tomorrow for Fredericksburg in order probably to discharge the last Act of *personal* duty, I may, (for her age) ever have it in my power to pay my Mother it would be very inconvenient for me."[56]

On March 8, 1789, George Washington visited his mother for the final time. The March 12, 1789 *Virginia Herald* recorded the visit, "On Saturday evening alt, His Excellency GERNERAL WASHINGTON arrived in town from Mount Vernon, and early on Monday morning he let out on his return. The object of his Excellency's visit was, probably, to take leave of his aged mother, sister and friends, previous to his departure for the New Congress,

[55] Ibid, 71.
[56] "From George Washington to Richard Conway, 6 March 1789," Founders Online, https://founders.archives.gov/?q=Mary%20Washington%20%20Author%3A%22Washington%2C%20George%22%201787&s=1111311111&sa=&r=69&sr=%20 (accessed October 26, 1789).

over the councils of which the united voice of America has called him to preside."[57]

According to family legend, during the final meeting between George Washington and his mother, George asked for her blessing. "You will see me no more," Mary Washington is said to have told her son. "My great age and the disease that is rapidly approaching my vitals warn me that I shall not be long for the world. I trust in God. I am prepared for a better. But go, George, and fulfil the high destiny which Heaven appears to assign you. Go, my son, and may that Heaven and your mother's blessing be always with you," Mary Washington is said to have instructed her son.[58]

Following George Washington's visit to his mother in the spring of 1789, it became clear that Mary Washington was entering her final months. One of Mary's physicians, Dr. Elisha Hall, was a cousin of Dr. Benjamin Rush, signer of the Declaration of Independence. Dr. Hall solicited the opinion of his cousin on the proper care for his patient. Dr. Hall concluded in a letter to his cousin on July 6, 1789, "The respectable age and character of your venerable patient lead me to regret that it is not in my power to suggest a remedy for the disorder you have described in her breast. I know nothing of the root you mention found in Carolina and Georgia, but, from a variety of inquiries, and experiments, I am disposed to believe there does not exist in the vegetable kingdom an antidote to cancer…Continue the application of opium and

[57] Felder, *George Washington's Fredericksburg*, 72.
[58] Ella Bassett Washington, "The Mother and Birthplace of Washington," *The Century Magazine*, April 1892, Vol. XLIII. No.6, 841.

camphor, and wash it frequently with a decoction of red clover…and support the system with wine and bark…"[59]

In the summer of 1789, George Washington had been seriously ill. Despite her own illness, Mary Washington was focused on the wellbeing of her son. Betty Lewis wrote to her brother on July 24, 1789, updating him on their mother's condition, "I am sorry to inform you my Mother's Breast still Continues bad. God only knows how it will end, I dread the consequence. she is sensible of it & is Perfectly resign'd—wishes for nothing more than to keep it Easy—she wishes to here from you, she will not believe you are well till she has it from under your Hand—the Doctors think it they could get some Hemloc [hemlock] it would be of Service to her Breast, if you Could Procure som there. Mr Urquhart will bring it for her, there is none to be got hear."[60]

The search for a cure proved fruitless. Mary Washington died on August 25, 1789, at her home in Fredericksburg. George Washington's nephew Burgess Ball wrote to the President to inform him on the death of his mother:

> "I am sorry that it devolvs on me to communicate to you the loss of your Mother who departed this Life abt 3 oClock today. The Cause of her desolution (I believe) was the Cancer on

[59] "'This Melancholy Call': Cancer in the Washington Family," George Washington's Mount Vernon, http://www.mountvernon.org/george-washington/cancer/ (accessed October 26, 2017).

[60] "To George Washington from Betty Lewis, 24 July 1789," Founders Online, https://founders.archives.gov/documents/Washington/05-03-02-0167 (accessed October 26, 2017).

her Breast, but for abt 15 days she has been deprived of her speech, and for the last five days she has remain'd in a Sleep.

She has lived a good Age &, I hope, is gone to a happier place than we live at present in. Mrs. Lewis being in much trouble, and all her Sons absent, she requested I wd [would] write to you on the Subject, and, as it may be necessary for you also to be acquainted with the last Will of the Old Lady, I herewith inclose a Copy thereof…"[61]

It took five days for Burgess Ball's letter to arrive in New York arriving on September 1, 1789. Robert Lewis, the President's nephew and secretary, recorded the moment the letter from Fredericksburg arrived in his journal.

"Baron Steuben and Govr. St. Clair dined with us to day—the Baron was remarkably cheerful and facetious, likewise greatly devoted to the President. In

---

[61] "To George Washington from Burgess Ball, 25 August 1789," Founders Online, https://founders.archives.gov/documents/Washington/05-03-02-0312 (accessed October 26, 2017).

the midst of our mirth my Uncle receiv'd a letter from Colo. Ball, informing of the death of my Grandmother; and event so long expecd could not create so much uneasiness as person less advanced in life. I am solicitous to hear from home. My apprehensions for the health of my Mother is great, knowing how attentive she was always during the Indisposition of the Old Lady." [62]

Several days later, on September 13, 1789, President Washington wrote to his sister Betty Lewis to offer his condolences and instructions on the disposal of their mother's estate:

"Colonel Ball's letter gave me the first account of my Mother's death—since that I have received Mrs Carter's letter written at your request—and previous to both I was prepared for the event by some advices of her

[62] Robert Lewis, "Diary, 4 July 1789 to 1 September 1789," 68-69, Digital Collections from the Washington Library, http://catalog.mountvernon.org/cdm/compoundobject/collection/p16829coll14/id/37/rec/6, accessed October 26, 2017).

illness communicated to your Son Robert.

Awful, and affecting as the death of a Parent is, there is consolation in knowing that Heaven has spared our to an age, beyond which few attain, and favored her with the full enjoyment of her mental faculties, and as much bodily strength as usually falls to the lot of four score. Under these considerations and a hope that she is translated to a happier place, it is the duty of her relatives to yield due submission to the decrees of the Creator—When I was last at Fredericksburg, I took a final leave of my Mother, never expecting to see her more

It will be impossible for me at this distance, and circumstanced as I am, to give the smallest attention to the execution of her will. Nor indeed is much required if, as she directs, no security should be given or appraisement made of her estate; but that the same should be allotted to the Devisees with as little trouble and delay as may be…"[63]

In regard to the items left to him by his mother in her will, George Washington commented,

"Were it not that the specific legacies which are given to me by the Will are meant, and ought to be considered and received as mementos of parental affection, in the last solemn act of life, I should not be desirous of receiving or removing them, but in this point of view I set a value on them much beyond their intrinsic worth."[64]

Since moving to Fredericksburg in 1772, George Washington had provided his mother with financial support. He assured Betty Lewis that he did not want reimbursement from his mother's estate.

---

[63] "From George Washington to Betty Washington Lewis, 13 September 1789," Founders Online, https://founders.archives.gov/?q=betty%20lewis%20Author%3A%22Washington%2C%20George%22%20&s=1111311111&sa=&r=51&sr=%20, (accessed October 26, 2017).
[64] Ibid.

"She has had a great deal of money from me at times, as can be made appear by my books, and the accounts of Mr L[und] Washington during my absence—and over and above this has not only had all that was ever made from the Plantation but got her provisions and every thing else she thought proper from thence. In short to the best of my recollection I have never in my life received a copper from the estate—and have paid many hundred pounds (first and last) to her in cash—However I want no retribution—I conceived it be a duty whenever she asked for money, and I had it, to furnish her notwithstanding she got all the crops or the amount of them, and took every thing she wanted from the planation for the support of her family, horses & ca besides," George Washington wrote to Betty

Lewis on September 13, 1789.[65]

George Washington went into official mourning upon receiving word of his mother's death. The president ordered "mourning Cockades & Ribbon" for all members of his household to wear. The president officially mourned his mother for five months. High ranking members of the federal government in New York went into mourning for Mary Washington for five weeks.[66]

Following Mary Washington's death, Betty Washington was tasked with burying her mother in a manner befitting the status of the Washington family. In the ledger detailing Mary Washington's final expenses, Joseph Berry, the town crier, was paid £1.15.0 for "carrying messages and Tolling the Bell."[67] Following Mary Washington's death, Joseph Berry as the town crier would have rung the bell at St. George's Episcopal Church which announced to the community that there had been a death. Because Mary was a woman, Joseph Berry would have rung the bell twice, then he paused briefly, then rung the bell for each year of Mary's life. Because Mary was a prominent member of the community, Joseph Berry would again ring the bell of St. George's in the same manner on the day of her funeral. He also assisted the family by delivering messages to members of the community alerting them to Mary's death and finalizing funeral and burial arrangements.

---

[65] Ibid.

[66] "Mary Ball Washington," George Washington's Mount Vernon, http://www.mountvernon.org/digital-encyclopedia/article/mary-ball-washington/ (accessed October 26, 2017).

[67] "Acct of the Estate of Mary Washington," Central Rappahannock Regional Library, Virginiana Room.

Funerals in 18th-century Virginia could be elaborate affairs, particularly if the deceased was a member of the gentry. Mary Washington's burial reflected her status as the respected matron of the Washington family. Her coffin was made by James Allen a prominent Fredericksburg furniture maker for the price of £8.6.4.[68] The coffin would have been made from mahogany lined in fine black wool. The price of the coffin suggests that the coffin was lead lined and might have had a brass name plate. Final funeral expenses paid to Betty Lewis from her mother's estate was £3.2.0.[69] Only members of the gentry could afford such an elaborate funeral and burial.

Mary Washington's obituary in the August 27, 1789 issue of the *Virginia Herald* noted

> "On Tuesday the 25th inst. died at her house in this town, Mrs. MARY WASHINGTON, aged 82 years, the venerable mother of the illustrious President of the United States, after a long and painful indisposition, which she bore with uncommon patience.— Tho' the pious tear of duty, affection and esteem, is due to the memory of so revered a character, yet our grief must be greatly alleviated

[68] Ibid.
[69] Ibid.

from the consideration that she is relieved from all the pitiable infirmities attendant on an extreme old age.—It is usual when virtuous and conspicuous persons quit this abode, to publish an elaborate panegyric on their character—suffice it to say, she conducted herself through this transitory life, with virtue, prudence and christianity, worthy the mother of the greatest hero that ever adorned the annuals of history."[70]

Mary Washington's obituary was carried in newspapers across the country. The *Gazette of the United-States* on September 9, 1789 published an epitaph for Mary Washington:

> *"O may kind heaven, propitious to our fate,*
>
> *Extend* THAT HERO'S *to* her *lengthen'd date;*
>
> *Through the long period* healthy, active, sage;

---

[70] Felder, *George Washington's Fredericksburg*, 72.

*Nor know the sad infirmities
of age.*"[71]

Following Mary Washington's death, Betty Lewis struggled to pay for her late mother's medical care. On October 1, 1789, Betty Lewis wrote to George Washington, "the Doctors bills is more than I expectted, [Dr. Elisha] Halls Bill is £45 P.— Mortemores [Dr. Charles Mortimer] £22P. the Debts I think will be upwards of one Hundred Pounds..."[72] In the ledger recording Mary Washington's estate, the final payment to Dr. Elisha Hall was £48.0.0 and the final payment to Dr. Charles Mortimer was £19.19.6, a vast sum for the 18th-century.[73] To pay the expenses Mary Washington accrued during her illness, Betty Lewis was forced to sell her mother's personal property not listed in her mother's will. On October 15, 1789, an ad was placed in the *Virginia Herald* alerting the community that Mary Washington's possessions were to be sold at auction. "On Thursday, the 29th instant, will be sold at the plantation, about 4 miles below this town, late the property of Mrs. Washington, deceased, all stocks of horses, cattle, sheep and hogs, planation utensils of every kind, carts, hay and fodder. That trouble of collection etc. [may be] avoided, they will be sold to the highest bidder, for ready money. All persons having claims against the deceased are required to

[71] *Gazette of the United-States*, September 9, 1789, 3, Chronicling American, http://chroniclingamerica.loc.gov/lccn/sn83030483/1789-09-09/ed-1/seq-3/ (accessed October 26, 2017).
[72] "'This Melancholy Call': Cancer in the Washington Family," George Washington's Mount Vernon, http://www.mountvernon.org/george-washington/cancer/ (accessed October 26, 2017).
[73] "Acct of the Estate of Mary Washington," Central Rappahannock Regional Library, Virginiana Room.

bring them in [to be] properly attended to," Betty Lewis wrote in the notice.[74]

According to family tradition, Mary Washington was buried near Meditation Rock on the Lewis plantation. Meditation Rock was Mary's favorite place to pray and she would visit the spot daily.

> "Always pious, in her latter days her devotions were performed in private. She was in the habit of repairing every day to a secluded spot, formed by rocks and trees near her dwelling, where, abstracted from the world and worldly things, she communed with her Creator in humiliation and prayer," George Washington Parke Custis remembered.[75]

The exact location of her final resting place has been lost to history.

From the age of three to the day that she died, Mary Washington was a slave owner. Little is known about the lives of the men and women who helped Mary run her house and care for her throughout her final illness. In bits and pieces, some of the experiences of her enslaved workers can be pieced together. During the Revolutionary War, Mary Washington requested that

---

[74] *Virginia Herald*, October 15, 1789, Central Rappahannock Regional Library, Virginiana Room.
[75] Custis, 141.

Lund Washington, who was managing Mount Vernon in General Washington's absences, send to Fredericksburg a slave woman called Silla. Lund Washington wrote back that Silla was unlikely to agree to the arrangement as she was married to Jack and "they appear to live comfortable together." Two weeks later, Lund Washington wrote to Mary Washington that he was "very sorry to part her from Jack. He cries and begs, saying he had rather be hanged than separated." Silla was sent to Fredericksburg to work for Mary Washington, but the arrangement only lasted a year. George Washington intervened and instructed Lund Washington, "In order to gratify Jack you may bring Silla up again."[76]

One of Mary Washington's slaves, George, was rented to George Washington to work at Mount Vernon in the 1770s. George worked in Mount Vernon's gardens. While at Mount Vernon, George married Sall Twine, who belonged to Martha Washington. By 1786 George had fathered three children with Sall. George Washington wished to keep George at Mount Vernon and wrote to his mother in 1787 that the slave, "will not, as he has formed connections in this neighborhood, leave it, as experience has proved him I will hire."[77] After Mary Washington's death, George Washington expressed his concern to Betty Lewis about George's future at Mount Vernon.

"Whilst it occurs to me, it is necessary it should be known that there is a fellow belonging to that estate now

---

[76] Marfé Ferguson Delano, *Master George's People: George Washington, His Slaves, and His Revolutionary Transformation* (Washington, D.C.: National Geographic, 2013), 25-26.

[77] Susan P. Schoelwer, *Lives Bound Together: Slavery at George Washington's Mount Vernon* (Mount Vernon Ladies' Association), 49.

at my house, who never stayed elsewhere, for which reason, and because he has a family I should be glad to keep him—He must I should conceive be far short in value of the fifth of the other negroes which will be to be divided, but I shall be content to take him as my proportion of them—and, if from a misconception either of the number of the value of these negroes it should be found that he is of greater value than falls to my lot I shall readily allow the difference, in order that the fellow may be gratified as he never would consent to go from me," George Washington wrote on September 13, 1789.[78]

In her will, Mary Washington left George to her son. George was freed by George Washington's will, but his wife and seven children were not freed as they belonged to the estate of Martha Washington's first husband. George's future after 1799 is

---

[78] "From George Washington to Betty Washington Lewis, 13 September 1789," Founders Online, https://founders.archives.gov/?q=betty%20lewis%20Author%3A%22Washington%2C%20George%22%20&s=1111311111&sa=&r=51&sr=%20, (accessed October 26, 2017).

unknown.[79] The other five slaves owned by Mary Washington mentioned in her will were all given to members of her family, their whereabouts after 1789 are unknown.

Mary Washington was remembered by her family as a loving woman. George Washington's cousin, Lawrence Washington, in his old age remembered his aunt as a formidable but kind woman.

> "I was often there with George, his playmate, schoolmate, and a young man's companion. Of the mother I was ten times more afraid than I ever was of my parents. She awed me in the midst of her kindness, for she was indeed, truly kind. I have often been present with her sons, proper tall fellows too, and we were all mute as mice; and even now, when time has whitened my locks…I could not behold that remarkable woman without feelings it is impossible to describe. Whoever has seen that awe-inspiring air and manner so characteristic in the Father of

---

[79] Schoelwer, 49.

his Country, will remember
the matron." [80]

Mary Washington's grandson Robert Lewis passed down to his family fond memories of his grandmother. Robert Lewis remembered the walks his siblings would take with Mary Washington on the Lewis plantation to Meditation Rock. "In later years Major Lewis often reverted to them as among his most interesting and pleasant recollections of his grandmother," descendent Ella Basset Washington wrote in 1892.[81] Robert Lewis remembered that his grandmother would instruct the Lewis children in lessons of natural history and the Bible during those rambles. According to Robert Lewis, Mary Washington's favorite Bible story to teach her grandchildren was the story of the deluge from the Book of Genesis. During the lessons, she would point out the changes to nature produced by the flood. "As one of them related when himself growing old, 'There was a spell over them as they looked into grandmother's uplifted face, with its sweet expression of perfect peace,' and they 'were very quiet' during the homeward walk," Ella Basset Washington recorded.[82]

In his memoir of his step grandfather, George Washington Parke Custis remembered Mary Washington as an industrious woman in his memoirs. "During the war, and indeed during her useful life, and until within three years of her death, when an afflictive disease prevented exertion, the mother of Washington set a most valuable example in the management of her domestic concerns, carrying her own keys, bustling in her household affairs,

---

[80] Custis, 131.
[81] Washington, 837.
[82] Ibid.

providing for her own wants, and living and moving in all the pride of independence."

While George Washington Parke Custis remembered Mary Washington for her industry, his sister Nellie Parke Custis Lewis remembered her for her simplicity, writing on March 16, 1851:

"I do not believe the Genl's mother ever had her likeness taken by any one—and certainly if it ever had been taken, her *children* and not strangers would have possessed it. The Genl. was her *eldest* son, Mr. Lewis's mother her *only* daughter— both favorites and both devoted to her—how then can it be supposed that a likeness of her could be *spared* by either of them. Mr. [Lawrence] L[ewis][83] was her favorite Grandchild, more with her than any other—he never *saw* or *heard* of any likeness being taken. She resembled the General Very much, I have heard an old companion of his Boyhood who was

---

[83] Lawrence Lewis (1767-1839), son of Fielding Lewis and Betty Washington Lewis married George Washington's step-granddaughter in 1799.

frequently at his mothers say, that she inspired as much *awe* as her son did, kind as she was always, he was more afraid of her than of any one he ever knew. She was always remarkably *plain* in her dress—I do not believe she ever *had*, much less *wore* a Diamond ring. I have never seen one in her family. The whole style of the dress was not of her...I was in mourning for her in New York; had a likeness of her been *above ground*, it would have been in her children's possession at that time."[84]

Mary Ball Washington was a remarkable woman. Born in an era in which women had few opportunities, she rose above the tragedies that shaped her early life to develop strength of character. These characteristics she passed down to her children, in particular that of her eldest son George Washington. Like all humans, Mary Washington was complex. She could be stubborn and her refusal to move in with one of her children during her final illness proved her frustrating to her children. Her political sympathies during the American Revolution are unclear and her apparent silence on the great political matters of the day has been difficult to modern scholars to understand. But she also displayed a loving nature

---

[84] "Transcript Nellie Custis Lewis, March 16, 1851," Mary Washington House archives.

towards her children. Through the few surviving letters she displayed flashes of humor even in the midst of the darkest days of the Revolution and a deep love for her family. What is striking to the modern observer is what those who actually knew Mary Washington remembered about her. Instead of discussions of her stance on American independence, Mary Washington's grandchildren remembered a loving and kind woman who they deeply loved and respected. This is the Mary Washington that should be remembered.

The Will of Mary Washington

As Registered in the Clerk's Office at Fredericksburg, Virginia

In the name of God! Amen. I, Mary Washington, of Fredericksburg, in the County of Spotsylvania, being in good health, but calling to mind the uncertainty of this life, and willing to dispose of what remains of my worldly estate, do make and publish this, my last will, recommending my soul in the hands of my Creator, hoping for a remission of all my sins through the merits and mediation of Jesus Christ, the Saviour of mankind; I dispose of my wordly estate as follows:

Imprimis.—I give to my son, General George Washington, all my land in Accokeek Run, in the County of Stafford, and also my negro boy George, to him and his heirs forever. Also my best bed, bedstead, and Virginia cloth curtains (the same that stand in my best bedroom), my quilted blue-and-white quilt, and my best dressing glass.

Item.—I give and devise to my son, Charles Washington, my negro man, Tom, to him and his assigns forever.

Item.—I give and devise to my daughter, Betty Lewis, my phaeton and bay horse.

Item.—I give and devise to my daughter-in-law, Hannah Washington, my purple cloth cloak lined with shag.

Item.—I give and devise to my grandson, Corbin Washington, my negro wench, old Bet, my riding chair, and two black horses, to him and his assigns forever.

Item.—I give and devise to my grandson, Fielding Lewis, my negro man, Frederick, to him and his assigns forever: also eight silver tablespoons, half my crockery ware and the blue and white tea china, with book case, oval table, one bedstead, one pair sheets, one pair blankets and white cotton counterpane, two table cloths, six red leather chairs, half my pewter and one-half of my iron kitchen furniture.

Item.—I give and devise to my grandson, Lawrence Lewis, my negro wench, Lydia, to him and his assigns forever.

Item.—I give and devise to my granddaughter, Betty Carter, my negro woman, little Bet, and her future increase, to her and her assigns forever; also my largest looking glass, my walnut writing desk with drawers, a square dining table, one bed, bedstead, bolster, one pillow, one blanket and pair of sheets, white Virginia cloth counterpane and purple curtains, my red-and-white tea china, teaspoons, and the other half of my pewter, crockery ware, and the remainder of my iron kitchen furniture.

Item.—I give to my grandson, George Washington, my next best dressing glass, one bed, bedstead, bolster, one pillow, one pair sheets, one blanket and counterpane.

Item.—I devise all my wearing apparel to be equally divided between my granddaughters, Betty Carter, Fannie Ball, and Milly Washington; but should my daughter, Betty Lewis, fancy any one, two or three articles, she is to have them before a division thereof.

Lastly. I nominate and appoint my said son, General George Washington, executor of this, my will, and as I owe few or no debts, I direct my executor to give no security nor to appraise my estate, but desire the same may be allotted to my devisees, with as little trouble and delay as may be, desiring their acceptance thereof as all the token I now have to give them of my love for them.

In witness whereof, I have hereunto set my hand and seal this 20th day of May, 1788.

Mary Washington

Witness, John Ferneyhough.

Signed, sealed and published in our presence, and signed by us in the presence of the said Mary Washington, and at her desire.

J. Mercer.

Joseph Walker.

Acknowledgments

I would like to thank the following individuals and organizations who assisted me in the writing of this book.

At the Washington Heritage Museums, I wish to thank Anne Darron, Executive Director for providing support for this project. I would also like to thank Courtney Cutler, Office Manager, who provided valuable feedback on this manuscript.

At the Mary Washington House, I wish to thank my wonderful guides who have fueled my research. I am deeply grateful to Jan Swagger, volunteer gift shop buyer, who prodded me on to complete this project.

At the University of Mary Washington, I wish to thank Michael Spencer, Associate Professor and Director of the Center for Historic Preservation, who has been very generous with his time and knowledge of 18th-century structures.

At the George Washington Foundation, I wish to thank Laura Galke, Small Finds Analyst, for her assistance and valuable feedback on this project. Her admiration for Mary Washington is infectious and inspired me in my work. I would also like to thank Meghan Budinger, Curator, for assisting my search for primary sources.

At the Central Rappahannock Regional Library Viginiana Room, I wish to thank Nancy Moore and Marian McCabe who provided me with assistance in uncovering valuable primary sources.

At George Washington's Mount Vernon, I wish to thank Amanda C. Isaac, Associate Curator, who was gracious with her time and knowledge answering my questions and providing source material on a variety of topics. I would also like to thank Mary V. Thompson, Research Historian, for her assistance. I must also thank Sarah Myers, Access Services Librarian, for providing information on the fate of Mary Washington's slaves.

At the Colonial Williamsburg Foundation, I wish to thank D.A. Saguto, Master Boot and Shoe Maker, and the interpreters of the Historic Trades Department for their assistance.

At the Fredericksburg and Spotsylvania National Military Park, I wish to thank John Hennessy, Superintendent, who generously provided information about the Mary Washington House in the 19th-century.

I must also thank my parents for their support and love.

About The Author

Michelle L. Hamilton earned her master's degree in history from San Diego State University in 2013. She is a lifelong student of history.

Michelle's other works include: *"I Would Still Be Drowned In Tears"* Spiritualism in Abraham Lincoln White House.

"My Heart Is In The Cause" The Civil War Diary of James Meyers – Hospital Steward 45th Pennsylvania 1863-1865

"Manners During The Civil War: American Etiquette Or The Customs Adopted By Polite Society Throughout The United States"

Hamilton currently serves as the manager of the Mary Washington House Museum in Fredericksburg, VA. She is not new to historical house museums as she also worked as a docent at The Whaley House Museum in Old Town San Diego from 2001 until 2006.

She has been a Civil War living historian for over a decade participating in Civil War living history events around California and Virginia. Additionally, she has been a requested speaker at several Civil War Roundtable meetings, radio talk shows and numerous magazine publications including "The Citizen's Companion"

See her list of other publications and request a copy from her website: www.MichelleLHamilton.net

Enjoy her blog at: http://michelle-hamilton.blogspot.com

www.ingramcontent.com/pod-product-compliance
Lightning Source LLC
Chambersburg PA
CBHW071103040426
42443CB00013B/3384